DIRECTIONS Starter 2

READING SKILLS

John Cooper

Oliver & Boyd

Contents

Introduction 3

1 *ALL IN ORDER* (The Alphabet) 5
   First Letter Order 6
   Second Letter Order 9

2 *LOOK IT UP* (The Dictionary) 10
   Arrangement of Words in a
     Dictionary 11
   Words at the Top of a Dictionary
     Page 15

3 *READ WITH SPEED* (Skimming) 17
   Scanning Lists 19
   Index 20
   Skimming Passages 21

4 *WHAT'S IT ALL ABOUT?*
   (Reading for Main Ideas) 22
   Sentences 25
   Paragraphs 26

5 *TELL ME MORE*
   (Supporting Details) 32
   Words and Pictures 32
   Paragraphs 37

6 *MATTER OF FACT*
   (Reading for Information) 39
   Pictographs 39
   Paragraphs 41
   At the Theatre 42

7 *THE REASON WHY*
   (Cause and Effect) 44

8 *STEP BY STEP*
   (Sequence and Instructions) 48
   Sequence 48
   Following Instructions 51
   Flow Chart 53
   Directions 54

9 *WHAT'S MISSING?*
   (Context Clues including Cloze
     Procedure) 55
   Pictures 55
   Sentences 56
   Paragraphs 56
   Clues to Meaning 58

10 *TAKE A HINT*
   (Inference and Prediction) 61
   Inference 61
   Prediction 63

Introduction

Directions 1 and *2* grew out of needs emphasised in the Bullock Report and Open University courses on Reading Development, made more immediate by requests from teachers attending in-service workshop sessions.

Neither book on its own could cater for the wide range of reading abilities in any one class. So *Directions Starter 1* and *2* have been produced to meet the demand for simpler material to cater for all levels of ability within a class. These books also make possible the introduction of this work to pupils at a relatively early age. Teachers may find it necessary at all levels, of course, to supplement the explanations and instructions in these books, which are often quite condensed on the assumption that they will be used in a teaching situation rather than solely for testing or mechanical practice.

Pupils who use this series will have learned to read. They will have mastered the basic decoding skills of identifying and pronouncing words and associating meanings with print. In order to read effectively, however, for enjoyment and for independent study, they must master more advanced reading skills and know when to use them. The skills developed through the *Directions* series are shown in the following table.

tional literacy in today's society. Before leaving primary school, pupils need to be able to use: reference books such as dictionaries and encyclopaedias; library resources such as topic and information books; "signposts" within a book, such as contents lists, indexes and headings; explanations and instructions such as those in textbooks, assignment cards and worksheets; techniques of inference and prediction, as in following a narrative or argument; evaluative processes, as in distinguishing between true and false, fact and opinion. They should also be introduced systematically to the reading demands of life outside school — the special requirements of, for example, a telephone directory, a street plan, a railway timetable, a recipe, a newspaper, an advertisement, a graph, chart or flow diagram.

For effective reading and independent study, all these skills must, of course, become automatic. For instance, it should not be necessary to spend an inordinate amount of study time locating a word in a dictionary; such time is better employed in studying the word's meaning, spelling or pronunciation. Practice exercises in these books are designed to help pupils find their way about a dictionary easily and rapidly. The format and arrangement of the dictionary are illustrated, alphabetical order is practised, and use of the guide words at the top of the page is demonstrated.

The skimming process involves similar rapid handling of printed text. The reader may

	Directions Starter 1	*Directions Starter 2*	*Directions 1*	*Directions 2*
Alphabetical Order	✓	✓	✓	✓
Skimming and Scanning	✓	✓	✓	✓
Reading for Main Ideas	✓	✓	✓	✓
Reading for Supporting Details	✓	✓	✓	✓
Reading for Information	✓	✓	✓	✓
Cause and Effect, Cohesion	✓	✓	✓	✓
Sequence and Instructions	✓	✓	✓	✓
Context Clues and Cloze Procedure	✓	✓	—	✓
Inference and Prediction	✓	✓	—	✓
Fact and Opinion	—	—	—	✓

The skills selected for practice in this series are those identified by teachers and researchers as necessary for successful mastery of learning materials in today's classrooms and for func-

need to locate a single word or name in an index, directory or passage of prose; he may wish to take in headlines and one or two general impressions; he may be refreshing his memory of a book or article. Many adults assert that without any instruction in the process of skimming, they nevertheless picked up this skill fortuitously. It is evident, however, that skimming techniques can be improved by practice of the kind given here. The danger identified by teachers of pupils skimming at the wrong time (eg when using mathematics or science workcards) highlights the need to be able to select the appropriate reading skill for the reader's particular purpose. The best way to develop such flexible reading strategies is through specific practice and application.

Much of our reading, whether for pleasure or study, involves information gathering. Clearly this will include not only skimming and scanning, but also a slower, more careful type of reading to digest the main points in the text. Pupils can be helped to recognise main ideas, first through pictures and lists (classification) and later by providing a number of suggestions from which the pupils make their choice. When readers can recognise main ideas and state them in their own words, they have taken a big step towards effective use of reading and mastery of print.

At this stage pupils should find it much easier to sort out the supporting details in a passage. This skill will help them in writing outlines and making notes. Lack of its mastery is probably one of the reasons why pupils tend to take straightforward copies from reference books when asked to do research in, for example, environmental studies. Pupils can be helped in applying this skill if they are asked to find a predetermined number of supporting details once the main idea has been established. It is a useful technique to pose a question relating to each required detail.

Sorting out subordinate detail will also help pupils to weigh up cause and effect — one of the key ideas binding history, geography and science together as environmental studies, for instance. Starting in the primary school, this skill needs to be developed through the kinds of activity offered in the first two books of the *Directions* series.

Young readers often have difficulty in understanding sequence, because the order of events in the text is not always the same as the order in which they actually happen. The relevance of the exercises on practising putting events in order is highlighted by those in following instructions. The latter demonstrate the need for a careful "reading for detail" followed by the ability to translate the instructions, in sequence, into action.

Exposure to new words and the ability to work out their meaning from clues in the text increases vocabulary. Cloze procedure exercises, like those in *Directions Starter 2* and *Directions 2*, are partly a training in looking for contextual clues. (The assessment aspect of cloze procedure is not dealt with here.) Just as pupils can find clues to words deleted, so they can learn to look for clues to the meaning of unfamiliar words. Admirable though the habit of checking meaning in a dictionary may be, it is not always possible to do so.

The greater the ability to make inferences, the more exciting reading can become. Writers often try to hold their readers' attention by inducing them to forecast events or make deductions from the evidence offered. The habit of making inferences and predicting outcomes will often increase interest in what is read; it may be no less exciting for the reader if he makes the wrong inference or predicts the wrong outcome. In books of this size it is only possible to give pupils a limited amount of practice in this skill and indicate possibilities to teacher and pupils.

In this media-centred age, it is vital for pupils to be able to distinguish opinion from fact. Although the distinction is not easy to demonstrate, since skilful selection of fact can clearly mould opinion, some practice is given in *Directions 2* in assessing factual presentations, slanted reports and advertisements.

The exercises in these books are not an end in themselves. The flexible reading strategies practised here should be applied in other learning situations. In these ways pupils are more likely to acquire the higher order reading skills necessary to make them more proficient — and happier — readers.

1. All in order
The Alphabet

You often have to find words in lists that are printed in alphabetical order (e.g. in a dictionary or index). Therefore, you need to know that alphabet well.

a b c d e f g h i j k l m n o p q r s t u v w x y z

What's next?

Below are five sections. Each section contains five lines of letters and in each line a letter is missing.
What are the missing letters?
Write them in your own book.
The first one is done for you each time.

1. a b – *Answer*: c
   d e –
   g h –
   j k –
   m n –

2. e f g – *Answer*: h
   i j k –
   m n o –
   q r s –
   u v w –

3. a b c d – *Answer*: e
   f g h i –
   k l m n –
   p q r s –
   u v w x –

In the next two sections the missing letter is not at the end of the line.

4. e f g h j k – *Answer*: i
   a b c d e f h
   g h i k l m n
   m n o p r s t
   s t u w x y z

5. a b c d f g h – *Answer*: e
   e f g h j k l
   k l m o p q r
   p q r t u v w
   u v w y z

5

a b c d e f g h i j k l m n o p q r s t u v w x y z

Put in order

Example: The letters *a b d c* are not written in alphabetical order. We can check from the alphabet and see the order should be *a b c d*.

Write the following letters in correct alphabetical order. Check with the alphabet at the top of the page if you are not sure.

A 1. f h g i
    2. m o n p
    3. p s q r
    4. r s u v t
    5. f g h j i

B 1. a f p m
    2. b e k g
    3. l w t z
    4. n k s v w
    5. j m p o r u

C 1. b a c f h
    2. f d e m o
    3. j l k p q
    4. e k g n p
    5. c d e i h
    6. h j i t v u
    7. b d c i k j s
    8. e g f o q p w
    9. a e d k o l p
   10. b e d n s r x

FIRST LETTER ORDER

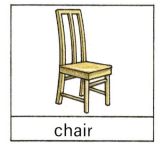
chair

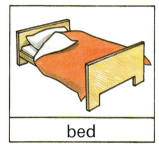
bed

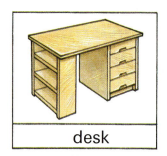
desk

Those three words are not in alphabetical order. Look at the first letters: *chair, bed, desk – c b d.*
The alphabetical order of the letters is *b c d.*
Therefore the alphabetical order of the words is: *bed, chair, desk.*

a b c d e f g h i j k l m n o p q r s t u v w x y z

Write the words in each section below in their alphabetical order.
(Remember to look at the first letter.
Check with the alphabet at the top of the page if necessary.)

1.
archer — boxer — diver — climber

2.
Fiona — Grace — Inga — Jean — Helen

3.
England
France
Holland
Italy
Germany

4.
kangaroo — lion — iguana — jackal

7

a b c d e f g h i j k l m n o p q r s t u v w x y z

Word Lists

Words are arranged in indexes and dictionaries in alphabetical order. You can often work out that order by looking carefully at the *first* letters of words.

Here are some lists of words for you to arrange in alphabetical order.
Example: *c*oat, *b*lazer, *h*at, *t*ie
   The first letters are: *c, b, h* and *t.*
   The alphabetical order of those letters is *b, c, h, t.*
   Therefore, the alphabetical order of the words is:
      *b*lazer, *c*oat, *h*at, *t*ie.

Write the following words in the correct alphabetical order.

A 1. buy   sell   rent
   2. stone   pebble   rock
   3. beneath   under   above
   4. book   magazine   comic   newspaper
   5. fairy   gnome   elf   imp

C 1. Fiona   Emma   Shirley   Janice
   2. Clive   Leslie   Andrew   Martin
   3. road   lane   street   pavement
   4. write   print   type   scribble
   5. hop   skip   jump   run

B 1. high   climb   view

   2. eat   food   drink

   3. play   tunes   band

   4. journey   rocket   land

8

a b c d e f g h i j k l m n o p q r s t u v w x y z

SECOND LETTER ORDER

Often we find more than one word in a list beginning with the same letter.

Example: run   race   Both words begin with *r*.

To put them in alphabetical order we must look at the second letters.   r**u**n   r**a**ce   u a   Alphabetical order is *a u*. Therefore, the alphabetical order of the words is:

   race   run

A   Are the words in the following pairs in alphabetical order?   Write yes or no each time.

   Example: mouse   man   *Answer:*   No

   1. act   age
   2. end   edge
   3. lie   look
   4. mouse   mink
   5. now   never

Write out each of the following lists in alphabetical order.   Remember to look carefully at the second letters.

B   1. ball   bounce   behind
   2. danger   disaster   despair
   3. hide   heave   haul
   4. knock   keep   kick
   5. James   John   Jean

C   1. hunt   herd   hill   hog
   2. flame   fire   foot   fun
   3. game   grass   girl   goal
   4. jam   jelly   junk   jotter
   5. lake   loaf   lump   list

D   1. mash   middle   meat   mule
   2. push   patch   plate   post
   3. rush   rent   rattle   roast
   4. scent   size   sole   sash
   5. tear   tire   turn   toss

2. Look it up
The Dictionary

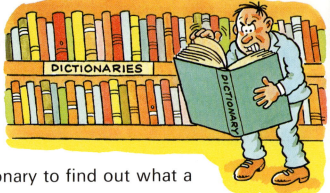

You often need to use a dictionary to find out what a word means.

Sometimes you may be able to work out the meaning of a new word from clues in the rest of the sentence.

Example:
Trevor was very disappointed because he missed the two early games, but he was *elated* when he played in the final and received a winner's medal.

You may not know what *elated* means but there are some clues. The sentence says he had been disappointed earlier but suggests that he is not so unhappy now. If he had received a winner's medal you would expect him to be *very delighted.* However, you should check from your dictionary just to make sure.

You can use a dictionary
(i) to look up new words,
(ii) to check the meaning of words you may have worked out from clues,
(iii) look up words whose meaning you may have forgotten,
(iv) to check the spelling of words.

ARRANGEMENT OF WORDS IN A DICTIONARY

Try this with your dictionary
(a) Open it near the beginning. Which letter do the words begin with?
(b) Open it about a quarter of the way through. Which letter do the words begin with?
(c) Open it about half-way through. Which letter do the words begin with?
(d) Open it about three-quarters of the way through. Which letter do the words begin with?
(e) Open it at the end. Which letter do the words begin with?

Words beginning A to D take up roughly the first quarter.   1st   A to D

Words beginning E to L take up roughly the second quarter.   2nd   E to L

Words beginning M to R take up roughly the third quarter.   3rd   M to R

Words beginning S to Z take up roughly the fourth quarter.   4th   S to Z

Draw four larger rectangles. Make them all the same size.

1st quarter — ABCD
2nd quarter
3rd quarter
4th quarter

In the first rectangle write all the starting letters of words you would find in the first quarter of the dictionary.

In the same way, write the correct letters in the other three rectangles you have drawn.

a b c d e f g h i j k l m n o p q r s t u v w x y z

It makes life easy if you can open the dictionary at about the right place for the word you want.

Remember! A dictionary is divided up roughly in this way.

In the *first quarter* words begin with letters A to D.
In the *second quarter* words begin with letters E to L.
In the *third quarter* words begin with letters M to R.
In the *fourth quarter* words begin with letters S to Z.

Which quarter?

A *For each of the following eight words write* first quarter, second quarter, third quarter *or* fourth quarter.

The first one is done for you. Check to see if the answer is correct.

1. orange   *Answer:* Third quarter, because O is in the third quarter (M to R).
2. blue   3. green   4. pink   5. white   6. violet
7. red   8. black

B *For each word write* first quarter, second quarter, third quarter *or* fourth quarter.
1. banana   2. grass   3. willow   4. pear
5. melon   6. fruit   7. yew   8. apple

C *In which quarter of the dictionary would you find each of the following?*
1. blackbird   2. pigeon   3. eagle   4. sparrow
5. robin   6. thrush   7. bluetit   8. wren
9. lapwing   10. magpie

a b c d e f g h i j k l m n o p q r s t u v w x y z

Backwards and forwards

You need to know the alphabet forwards, but you must also be able to work backwards.

Example: If you are looking up the word *muscular,* which begins with *m,* and you open your dictionary at a page with words beginning with *p,* you go backwards.

M N O P You go back 3 letters.

A In each of the following, should you go back or forward *each time?*
Write the answers in your own book.

	If you turn up words beginning with	and you are looking for words beginning with	you must turn?
Example	T	P	back
1	A	C	?
2	G	E	?
3	J	H	?
4	P	R	?

B In your own book write back *or* forward *for each of the following.*

	If you turn up words beginning with	and you are looking for words beginning with	you must turn?
Example	N	R	forward
1	B	A	?
2	D	G	?
3	F	E	?
4	H	K	?

a b c d e f g h i j k l m n o p q r s t u v w x y z

Write back *or* forward *for each.* Number 1 *is done for you.*

C

	If you turn up words beginning with	and you are looking for words beginning with	you must turn?
1	Z	V	back
2	F	C	?
3	M	Q	?
4	T	X	?
5	X	Z	?
6	G	K	?
7	P	F	?
8	Y	S	?
9	K	E	?
10	V	R	?

D

	If you turn up words beginning with	and you are looking for words beginning with	you must turn?
1	C	G	forward
2	L	E	?
3	O	J	?
4	E	H	?
5	R	M	?
6	U	N	?
7	H	L	?
8	N	F	?
9	I	G	?
10	Q	L	?

WORDS AT THE TOP OF A DICTIONARY PAGE

It is easy to tell which words are given on any page of the dictionary.

If you open your dictionary and look at the tops of the pages, you will find on each page two words and a number.

Example: ball   17   bear

The number **17** is the number of the page.
ball will be the first word on the page and you will be given the meaning.
bear will be the last word on the page, and you will be given the meaning.

Words which come between **ball** and **bear** will be on this page.
bark, barn, beach, bean would be on this page because they come between **ball** and **bear**.

A   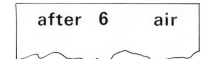   ajar   7   amber

Say whether each of the ten words below would appear on *page* **6** or *page* **7**, and why.
Write the answers in your own book.
Number 1 is done for you.
(Remember to look carefully at the second letter of each word.)

1. again   *Answer:* page 6 (because *ag* comes between *af* and *ai*)

2. alarm
3. agony
4. ahead
5. amaze
6. akin
7. aim
8. always
9. aid
10. ale

B

| ear 24 educate | eel 25 else | embark 26 engine |

On which pages would you find each of the following words?
Write the answers in your own book.

1. early
2. effect
3. egg
4. elder
5. eat
6. either
7. emerald
8. ebb
9. eject
10. ember
11. eight
12. echo
13. eerie
14. end
15. edge

C

| oak 76 octopus | odd 77 ointment | old 78 opium |

Write the number of the page on which you would find each of the following words.

1. obey
2. odour
3. open
4. omit
5. oil
6. onion
7. oar
8. olive
9. ogre
10. occur
11. ooze
12. ohm
13. once
14. observe
15. office

3. Read with speed
Skimming

Sometimes you can find out all you need to know without spending a long time studying the information closely.

Below are six questions about the picture.

To find each answer, glance very quickly over the picture. Try to find all six answers very quickly, and write them in your own book.

1. How many zebra crossings are there?
2. How many men do you see?
3. How many cars do you see?
4. How many clocks do you see?
5. How many flags are there?
6. How many wheels can you see?

Take your pick

Some people are very good at spotting just the item they want.
Here is some practice in this skill. You are looking for these eight items.

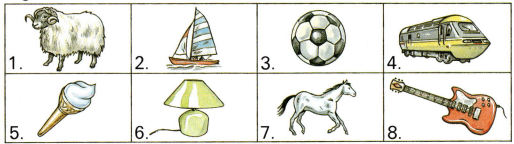

Each appears in one of the small pictures below.
Take one item at a time and glance over the pictures below to see how quickly you can spot the picture with the item you are looking for.

Number 1 is done for you.
We can write the answer as 1 (c) because item 1 appears in picture (c).

Do the others the same way.

SCANNING LISTS

Sometimes we need to find just one bit of information. We may not read every word carefully, but just glance over the print to find the important details. You can practise this skimming when you are looking for a word in a list.

Here is a list of names written in *four* columns – (a), (b), (c) and (d).

(a)	(b)	(c)	(d)
Agnes	David	Lawrie	Robert
Ahmed	Elizabeth	Lorna	Ross
Alice	Elma	Lucy	Sylvester
Andrew	Ernest	Mary	Thomas
Bruce	Evelyn	Maurice	Tracy
Charles	Henry	Nancy	Violet
Colin	John	Peter	William

A Each of the nine names below is in the list.
Check quickly to see which column.
Write the column – (a), (b), (c) or (d) – as your answer.
Example: Nancy *is in column* (c). *Answer:* (c).
Do the following nine in the same way as quickly as you can.

1. Bruce 2. Peter 3. John 4. Mary 5. Thomas
6. Evelyn 7. Charles 8. Henry 9. Violet

B Write down how many names start with each letter.
Example: Four names start with A. *Answer:* A4.

INDEX

Imagine you have a book about sweets. Part of its index is shown below.

Suppose you wished to find out about pandrops. You would glance quickly down the index until you came to the word *pandrops*. It tells you to turn to page 10 of the book.

Read each item below. Remember the word underlined. Skim over the index until you come to the word and then note down the page number. Write the answers in your own book.
(Number 1 is done for you.)

INDEX			
barley sugar	3	marshmallows	13
butterscotch	5	nougat	4
chocolate	1	pandrops	10
fudge	9	pastilles	2
humbugs	6	rock	7
jelly babies	8	toffee	12
liquorice	12		

If you wished to find out about   *You would turn to page*

1. how to make <u>butterscotch</u>   5
2. what <u>humbugs</u> are made of   ?
3. where <u>fudge</u> is made   ?
4. good quality <u>chocolate</u>   ?
5. the flavour of <u>marshmallows</u>   ?
6. varieties of <u>rock</u>   ?
7. what <u>jelly babies</u> are made of   ?
8. where <u>liquorice</u> is made   ?
9. good quality <u>nougat</u>   ?
10. the flavour of <u>barley sugar</u>   ?
11. different kinds of <u>toffee</u>   ?
12. where <u>pastilles</u> are made   ?

SKIMMING PASSAGES

When we are looking for a single piece of information in a passage we may skim through the text until we find it.

See how quickly you can spot the answers to the following questions in the passage below.

1. Who hurried up the road?
2. Who had given him the key?
3. Where did he dump the heavy canvas bag?
4. Where did he feel a draught?
5. What was wedged in the crack?

They said goodbye and she pushed open the gate. Ferdinand hurried away up the road in his old mackintosh, the hood over his head and the tail slapping against his legs like a wet fish. His mother had given him a key, and he carelessly left it on the outside of the door when he came in. He shook the raincoat, pulled out the damper in the stove, and dumped the heavy canvas bag he used as a satchel on the table. Then feeling a draught on the back of his legs, he looked over his shoulder at the door. It was slightly open and so he got up to shut it. But something was in the way, and looking down, Ferdinand saw with a start that there was the toe of a shoe wedged in the crack.

(From *A Hundred Million Francs* by Paul Berna)

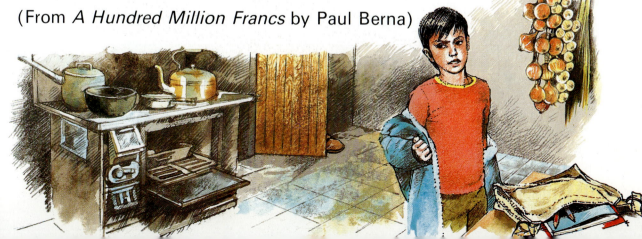

4. What's it all about?
Reading for Main Ideas

It is easier to understand and remember what we read if we can pick out the main ideas as we go along. Sometimes a heading or title tells us what we are reading about.
Below are four lines of drawings made by Tom. What was Tom drawing in each line?

In your own book write down what Tom was drawing in each line.

Titles

A Here are five titles:
(a) Colours, (b) Birds, (c) Hats, (d) Games, (e) Metals.

Try to match each title with the correct list below. The first one is done for you.
Write the answers in your own book.

		Title
1.	Copper, gold, silver	Metals
2.	Helmet, cap, turban	?
3.	Blue, yellow, green, purple	?
4.	Rugby, polo, tennis	?
5.	Seagull, sparrow, thrush	?

B What is the writer thinking about in each of the following lists?
Write down a suitable title or heading for each list.

1. Bungalow, flat, igloo
2. Canoe, dinghy, yacht
3. Shirts, trousers, vests
4. Apples, oranges, grapes
5. Lettuce, turnips, potatoes

Places

Example: Where would you find all of these: runways, aeroplanes, passengers, fire-engines?

Answer: airport.

Write down the place where you would be most likely to see each of the five groups of items below.

1. Hens, ducks, cows, sheep, pigs
2. Cages, lions, tigers, pool, penguins, polar bears
3. 22 players, referee, spectators, policemen
4. Doctors, nurses, operation tables, beds, patients
5. Sand, shells, seaweed, rocks

The Main Point—Pictures

Often we need to pick out the most important point from a number of ideas.
Each of the pictures on this page tells us more than one thing, but what is each picture *mainly* about?

Example: Look at the first picture. We can see:
(a) the bridge has broken under the weight of the lorry,
and (b) there is a swan in the water.
Answer: (a), the bridge is collapsing under the weight of the lorry.

A *Look at the picture. Write down in your own book the* main *thing it is telling us.*
Is it: (a) that the horse is almost at the winning post
or (b) that the jockey's cap has blown off?

B *Look at the picture. What is the* main *thing it is telling us?*
Is it: (a) that the sun is shining,
or (b) that the lion is escaping?

SENTENCES

What is the main thing the sentence is telling us?

Example: Harry was very happy to receive the watch, which was something he had never expected.

The sentence tells us (a) that the watch made Harry happy,

and (b) that he had never expected it.

Clearly the main thing it is telling us is

(a) that the watch made Harry happy.

Clean Teeth

Decide what is the most important thing each of the sentences below is telling us.

1. The school dentist advised all the pupils to clean their teeth every day, even those who said they did not eat sweets.
   What is the main thing this sentence tells us?
   Is it (a) that all were advised to clean their teeth daily,
   or (b) that some did not eat sweets?

2. Mary Meldrum cleaned hers every morning even when she did not have much time.
   What is the main thing this sentence tells us?
   (a) Mary Meldrum did not have much time some mornings.
   (b) Mary Meldrum cleaned her teeth every morning.

3. At the age of 12 Mary still had all her teeth which is more than could be said of her sister, Alice.
   What is the main thing this sentence tells us?
   (a) Mary still had all her teeth.
   (b) Mary had a sister called Alice.

25

PARAGRAPHS

When writing a paragraph a writer usually has a main idea in mind which he is telling us about.

James

In the paragraph below the writer mentions
    (a) James's saving
and (b) the price of sweets.

Read the paragraph and make up your own mind whether (a) James's saving *or* (b) the price of sweets *is the main idea the writer has in mind.*

James saved as much money as he could. He always spent as little as possible. When sweets went up in price he still saved money because he bought less. Every week he liked to count up his savings.

John's Holiday in Africa

Here are five main ideas.
(a) Lunch in a hotel   (b) Visit to Kenya
(c) Journey by air   (d) Visit to a game park
(e) Visit to Egypt.

Take the paragraphs opposite one at a time and see if you can find which of these five main ideas the writer had in mind each time.

Example: Paragraph 1 tells us about John's *journey by air.*
We can write the answer like this:
    1. (c) Journey by air.

Now pick the main ideas for paragraphs 2 to 5 opposite.

1. John set out on his first trip abroad by air. He was very excited because it was the fastest he had ever travelled.

2. The first stop was in Egypt. There, John had a car tour through Cairo, a ride on the back of a camel, and a quick visit to the Pyramids, where the ancient Pharaohs were buried.

3. Soon it was time to hurry to catch the plane again. It took them on to Kenya where they stayed the night in a hotel. This was lucky for John, because it gave him time to see the city of Nairobi, and also to go on a tour the next day.

4. John was up very early in the morning and arrived at a game park while it was still dark. At first light they hoped to see wild animals drinking at the water holes. John saw lions, elephants, zebras, antelopes and many other animals. Several times they were able to park the car only a few metres from the animals.

5. Before catching the plane again they had lunch in the hotel. John enjoyed it all but some of the dishes were strange to him. He had never heard of paw-paw before. Although he had heard of venison he had never tasted it, but when it came to ice-cream he felt much more at home.

The Green Sports Car

Here are three paragraphs about a car chase. Below each one are two suggestions as to what was the main idea in the writer's mind.

Read each paragraph and decide which is the main idea.

1. The green sports car crossed the red traffic lights. Too late Henry saw the danger and tried to swerve out of the way, but he was thrown on to the pavement. He got to his feet, almost in tears as he saw his motor cycle wrecked and the car speeding away.

This paragraph is mainly about
    (a) traffic lights
    (b) an accident.

2. The policemen outside the Town Hall had seen what had happened. Off they went in pursuit of the sports car. By the time they reached Hunter Road they were travelling at 100 km an hour and catching up quickly. More and more closely they crept up as they sped through Junction Road watched by hundreds of shoppers on the pavement.

This paragraph is mainly about
    (a) the chase
    (b) shoppers watching.

3. The green car screeched into Mile Grove and struck a lamp post, but before the driver could get away he was grabbed by the policemen. Although he said he did not know why they were chasing him, they held his arms tightly and pushed him towards the police car. There was little hope of escape.

This paragraph is mainly about
    (a) hitting the lamp post
    (b) the arrest.

Sheila

In this paragraph we shall find that the writer mentions
- (a) the weather in Scotland,
- (b) the poor bus service,

and (c) Sheila's love of cycling.

Read the paragraph and decide which one of the three is the main idea in the writer's mind.

Sheila's favourite way of travelling was on her bicycle. She cycled hundreds of kilometres on holiday in Scotland even though the weather was poor. Nearly every day she cycled to work because there were very few buses, and in her spare time she often cycled just to keep herself fit.

Artistic Twins

Here are two paragraphs about the twins, Herbert and Ann Clark.

Write in your own book what each paragraph is mainly about.

1. Herbert Clark and his twin sister, Ann, loved painting. When their mother bought them painting sets, they were so happy painting that they did nothing else all day.

Paragraph 1 is mainly about . . . ?

2. But Mrs Clark soon became very angry with them. When she was out shopping, they had started to paint a picture on the wall. Their mother was furious and said there was to be no more painting.

Paragraph 2 is mainly about . . . ?

5. Tell me more
Supporting Details

Picking out the main idea often helps us to see how the other details fit into place.

▪ WORDS AND PICTURES

There are four pictures below and on the opposite page. Write down in your own book the most suitable title from the following list for each picture.

(a) At the top of Mont Blanc
(b) Fishing
(c) Rainy day
(d) Car race

Perhaps you found it easy to select the title for each picture. Of course, you will have noted some of the details in each picture too. The questions that follow will help you to pick out some of the details in each picture.

Now study Picture 1 and answer the three questions on it.

Picture 1 (a) How many cars altogether can you see in the race?
(b) How many cars are damaged?
(c) How many stewards with flags can you see?

Do Pictures 2, 3 and 4 the same way.

Picture 2   (a) How many climbers are in the picture?
            (b) How many flags are flying at the top?
            (c) How many helicopters are there in the picture?

Picture 3   (a) How many ladies are carrying umbrellas?
            (b) How many men are wearing hats?
            (c) How many children are sheltering in the shop doorway?

Picture 4   (a) How many fishermen are on the river banks?
            (b) How many boats are in the river?
            (c) How many fish can you see?

Fill in the Details

Here are five puzzles. You are given a title for each one, but some of the details are left out.
Copy down what you are given and also write in the missing details.

1.   (a)   1967, 1972, 1975,   Calendar
    (b)   Monday, Wednesday, Saturday,   *Details* (a) Years
    (c)   March, April, June   (b) ?
                                                              (c) ?

2.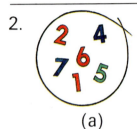
    (a)   (b)   (c)

    Sets
    Details (a) ?
            (b) ?
            (c) Signs

3.
    (a)   (b)

    Air Transport
    Details (a) ?
            (b) ?

4.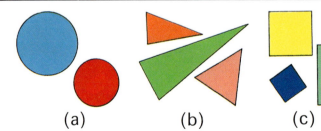
    (a)   (b)   (c)

    Shapes
    Details (a) ?
            (b) ?
            (c) ?

5.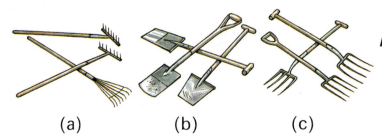
    (a)   (b)   (c)

    Garden Tools
    Details (a) ?
            (b) ?
            (c) ?

Details wanted

There are four sets of pictures on this page.
Copy down the title of each set and write in the three details.

Example: The title for the first set of pictures is: *Musical instruments.*

We see a violin, a guitar and a piano.

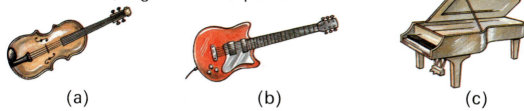

(a) (b) (c)

We can write our answer: 1. *Title* Musical instruments
Details (a) Violin, (b) Guitar, (c) Piano

Do the others in the same way.

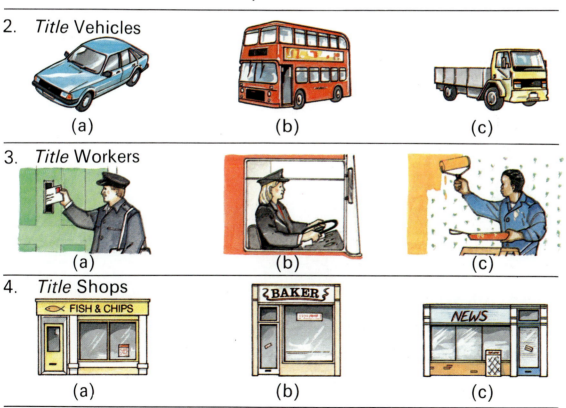

2. *Title* Vehicles
   (a) (b) (c)

3. *Title* Workers
   (a) (b) (c)

4. *Title* Shops
   (a) (b) (c)

35

What are they doing?

Here are three sets of pictures.
In each set you see Tom, Ross and William.
You are given the title for each set and asked to write down what each boy is doing.
Copy down the title each time and write underneath the details you are asked for. Part of Number 1 is done for you.

1. *Title* On the way to school
   (a) Tom is cycling.
   (b) Ross is?
   (c) William is?

(a) (b) (c)

2. *Title* At the seaside
   (a) Tom is?
   (b) Ross is?
   (c) William is?

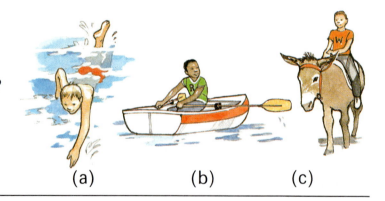

(a) (b) (c)

3. *Title* Playing in the snow
   (a) Tom is?
   (b) Ross is?
   (c) William is?

(a) (b) (c)

PARAGRAPHS
Give details

You are given the title for this paragraph. Copy it down and also write out the details.

Jane travelled by herself to visit her aunt in America. Crossing the Atlantic by plane was the easiest part of the journey. The bus journey from Kennedy Airport to the city centre was more confusing.

Title: Jane's journey to her aunt's
Details: (a) Across the Atlantic by?
        (b) To the city centre by?

Footprints in the snow

*Read the passage on the following page.
You are told below what the first three paragraphs are about but you are not told the details.
Read each paragraph again. Copy down the main ideas you are given and write in the missing details.*

1. The marks James saw in the snow.
    Details (a) ?
           (b) ?

2. The things James found left in the shed.
    Details (a) ?
           (b) ?
           (c) ?

3. James found no one in the hut.
   (*Where did he search?*)   (a) ?
                                      (b) ?

1. As James looked out at the white landscape his eye fell on the marks in the snow. A set of footprints led from the trees, past the garden gate and up to the door of the shed. Beside the footprints were two parallel lines, very possibly made by the runners of a sledge.

2. Cautiously he went out to the shed and pushed the door open. Sure enough there was a sledge which was soaking wet and had been left behind the door. Near the window he could see an open haversack and on the bench was a pair of gauntlet gloves.

3. But he could see no one. Slowly he went inside and looked around. Underneath the bench nothing had been disturbed. For a moment he paused and looked at the tall wooden cupboard. The door had been locked from the outside but, just to make sure, he opened it. There was no sign of life. Satisfied that the hut was deserted, James walked out through the door.

4. Suddenly he stopped. There was an unmistakable creak in the roof.

6. Matter of fact
Reading for Information

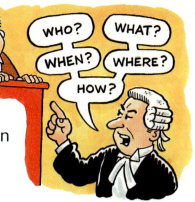

We all have to read a lot of information. This often means paying close attention to every detail.

PICTOGRAPHS

Games played by young people living in King Street

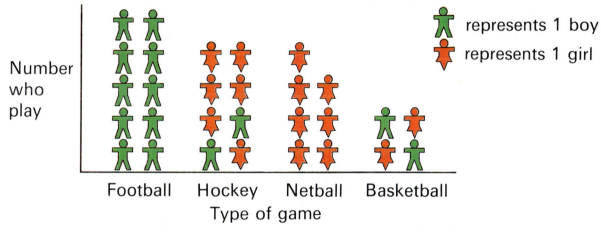

Read each of the following statements carefully. Next, study the pictograph to see whether each statement is true, or false or whether the pictograph doesn't say.

(Number 1 is done for you but check to see if the answer is correct.)

	Answer
1. The boys do not play netball. (If you look carefully at the pictograph you will see there are no boys in the netball column. This statement is true.)	1. True
2. Football is the most popular game mentioned.	2. ?
3. Hockey is the least popular of the four games.	3. ?
4. The same number play netball as play hockey.	4. ?
5. The oldest boys and girls play hockey.	5. ?

Money money

On this page another type of pictograph gives us information about spending money.
To get the correct information we must study it in *detail.*

How Ian spent his birthday money

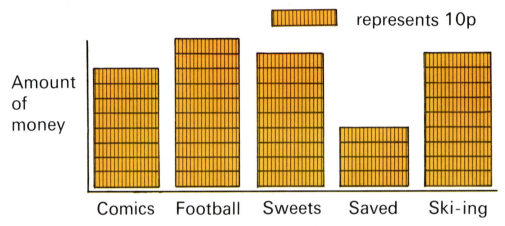

Read the eight statements. *Next, check up from the pictograph to see whether each statement is* true, false, *or* doesn't say, *and write down your answer.*
(Number 1 is done for you.   Check to see if it is correct before you copy it down.)

	Answers
1. Ian's birthday is in March. (The pictograph does not tell us.)	1. Doesn't say
2. Ian spent 80p on comics.	2. ?
3. Ian spent more on football matches than he spent on ski-ing.	3. ?
4. He spent 90p on sweets.	4. ?
5. It was Ian's mother who told him to save money.	5. ?
6. He saved only 40p.	6. ?
7. There were big crowds at the football matches.	7. ?
8. Ian spent the same amount on sweets as on comics.	8. ?

PARAGRAPHS

Madame Tussaud's travels

Below are three paragraphs. Before each paragraph are two statements.
Read the statements and then study the paragraph to find out whether each statement is true or not true or whether the paragraph doesn't say.

> *Example:* Madame Tussaud and her son set sail on a Sunday.
> *Answer:* Doesn't say

1. There were three storms between London and Leith.
2. The models which were smashed were the best models only.

Madame Tussaud and her son set sail for Scotland with her models. Three storms blew up between London and Leith. All the models were damaged and many were completely smashed. But the moulds, from which new models of the same type could be made, were safe.

3. Her son helped her to make new models.
4. She opened her exhibition three weeks after arriving in Edinburgh.

Day and night she worked hard to remake the collection of models. Although very tired, she was thrilled to be able to open an exhibition in Edinburgh eight days after arriving there.

5. She went to Glasgow before going to Ireland.
6. She did not know it was dangerous to travel by sea.

The exhibition was a great success. She went on to Glasgow. While she was there, she decided to go to Ireland although she knew it was dangerous to travel by sea at that time because there was war with France.

AT THE THEATRE

Sometimes it may be necessary to work out a lot of facts from information presented in unusual ways.

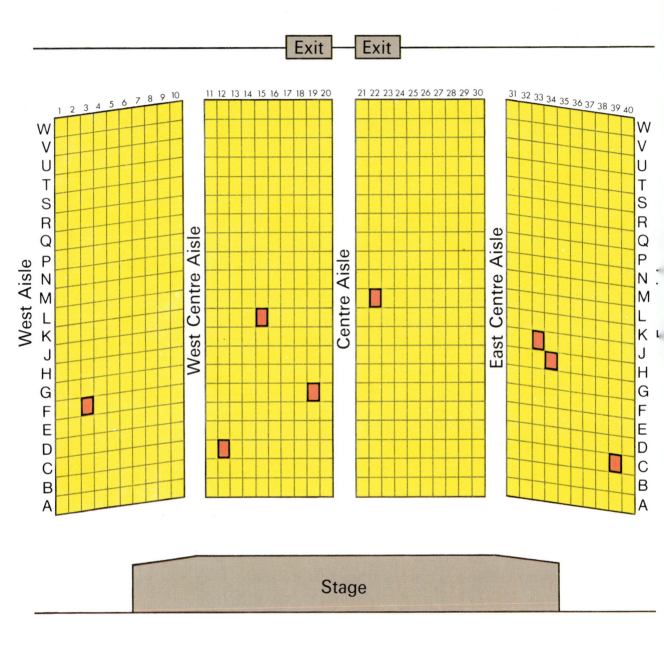

On the left is a plan of the seats in City Theatre. Albert, James, David, Alfred, Susan, Pauline, Mary and Jane went to the theatre on the same evening, but they could not get seats together. They had the seats marked ☐.

From the seating plan and the eight statements below work out where each of them sat. Write down your answers in your own book. (The first one is done for you.)

	Row	Number	
1. Albert had the seat nearest the east centre aisle.	J	33	Albert
2. Jane had a seat in the row in front of Albert.	H	?	Jane
3. Alfred had the seat nearest the west aisle.	?	?	Alfred
4. James had a seat in the same row as Alfred.	?	?	James
5. David had the seat nearest the exit.	?	?	David
6. Susan had the seat nearest the east aisle.	?	?	Susan
7. Mary had a seat in the same row as Susan.	?	?	Mary
8. Pauline had the seat furthest from an aisle.	?	?	Pauline

7. The reason why
Cause and Effect

It can be difficult to understand the reasons for some things. It helps if we can sort out causes and effects in our own minds.

Why do things happen?

Look at the pictures.   Think out an answer to each of these questions.
Write your answers in your own book.   (Number 1 is done for you.)

1. What caused the hole in the wall?   *(Picture 1)*
   Answer: The car ran into it.
2. Why are the trees leaning over?   *(Picture 2)*
3. What has caused the burglar to run away?   *(Picture 3)*
4. What is causing the bird to fly away?   *(Picture 4)*

Why?

Example: James had no money left. Why?
Answer: He had spent it all at the fair.

We could write the two sentences as one. James had no money left *because* he had spent it all at the fair.

Choose the best phrase from the box to complete the five sentences below. Write down the whole sentence in your own book.

1. John went to bed early because . . . .
2. Bob wrote with a biro pen because . . . .
3. Susan worked on Saturdays because . . . .
4. Tom started to wear glasses because . . . .
5. Nan took guitar lessons because . . . .

she needed money	he was tired
she hoped to join a band	he had lost his pencil
his eyesight was not good	

Mr Smith's journey

Join the following pairs of sentences together using the word because. *Think carefully whether to write* because *at the beginning or middle. Write the whole sentences in your own book.*

1. The train was late. Mr Smith missed the meeting.
2. He decided to return immediately. There was nothing useful he could do.
3. The return journey was very fast. The train was a new high speed type.
4. The last bus had gone. He walked home from the station.
5. He wished he had stayed at home. The whole journey had been a waste of time.

Lost?

Here are five questions beginning with *why*. You can find the answers by reading the passage below. Each of your answers will give the reason or cause.

1. Why could they not find the path?
2. Why did they have to get back soon?
3. Why were they rather worried?
4. Why was David quite happy?
5. Why did it not matter that they had lost the path?

Read the following passage and then answer the questions above.

Example: Answer 1 There had been more snow. (Do not write the word *because* each time.)

Tom and David could not find the path because there had been fresh falls of snow. It was important for them to be back soon as it was getting late. Their biggest worry was that they had no food left, but David was quite happy since he was sure they could be back within two hours. The path was not all that important in this area where there were no cliffs or very steep slopes.

End of term

Find the answer in the passage below to each of the five questions. Write out each answer in your own book.

1. Why was Gavin happy?
2. What was the reason for Bill being happy?
3. For what reason had they not been happy in the morning?
4. What was the reason for giving Miss Peters a lamp?
5. What was the cause of Miss Peters' retirement?

Gavin: I am looking forward to going away to Hilton Farm again this year. I am allowed to work with the hay and milk a cow.

Bill: That sounds exciting. But I am pleased to be having my holidays at home this year. Pierre, my pen friend from France, is coming to stay with me for three weeks. We are going to have a great time.

Gavin: I did not enjoy this morning.

Bill: Neither did I. I wish Miss Peters was not leaving. She has been our favourite teacher.

Gavin: She thought the lamp was a nice farewell present.

Bill: Yes. What a pity she has not been well. She said that if her health had been good, she would not have retired.

8. Step by step
Sequence and Instructions

▩ SEQUENCE

We have to be able to understand the order of some events – which comes first, which is next and so on.

Papering a Wall

Look carefully at the three pictures and the sentences underneath.

He spreads paste on the paper.

He sticks wallpaper on the wall.

He mixes the paste.

The order is wrong. Put them in the right order. What does he do first? What does he do next? What does he do last? Write out the sentences in the right order. (Do not draw the pictures.)

Picture Stories

*Look carefully at the pictures and the sentences underneath.
The order is wrong. What happened first? What happened next?
What happened last?
Write out the sentences in the right order. (Do not draw the
pictures.)*

A

On the evening of 5th November their father lit the fire.

On 1st November they collected wood and paper.

On 4th November they stacked up the wood and paper for the fire.

B *Do the same with these.*

Jane wraps up each present and writes the address label for each parcel.

Jane posts presents to her friends.

Jane goes to the shops to buy presents.

49

TV Aerial

The pictures (a), (b), (c) are in the wrong order. What is the right order of the pictures?

Order of events

The following sets of sentences are in the wrong order. Write them in the order in which the events would happen.

1. (a) When I get to school, we shall play outside until the assembly bell rings.
   (b) I shall run to school.
   (c) After school I shall come straight home today.
2. (a) She played the guitar in the school orchestra.
   (b) May went to lessons so that she could learn to play the guitar.
   (c) Mrs Brown bought her daughter, May, a guitar before she started lessons.
3. (a) Ronald was told on Wednesday that he would have to make a speech at the dinner on Friday.
   (b) His speech on the Friday evening was the best he had ever made.
   (c) He spent all Thursday afternoon preparing what he was going to say.

FOLLOWING INSTRUCTIONS

It is important to have things in the right order when we are following instructions.

Coffee break

Here are four instructions on how to operate the coffee machine, but they are in the wrong order.

> Wait until the machine fills the carton.
> Press the button for the type of coffee you wish.
> Take out the carton of coffee.
> Insert money in the slot.

Here are four pictures (a), (b), (c) and (d), showing the order the instructions should be in. *Write in your own book an instruction to match each picture. The first one is done for you.*

> (a) Insert money in the slot.

🟨 Don't Lose the Canary!

Each day Anne let her canary out of the cage to fly around the room.
Mother had given her some instructions to carry out before the canary was allowed out.

Here are five pictures showing the correct order.

Below are five instructions.

(a) Put out the cat   (b) Close the door
(c) Take canary out   (d) Close the window
(e) Open the cage.

Match an instruction to each picture.   The instruction for picture 1 is (d) so we can write the answer as 1 (d).
Write all five answers in your own book.

FLOW CHART

Don't Lose the Canary

In your own book copy down the flow chart on this page.
In each space write an instruction.   (Number 1 is done for you.)
for you.)
Try to get them all in the correct order.

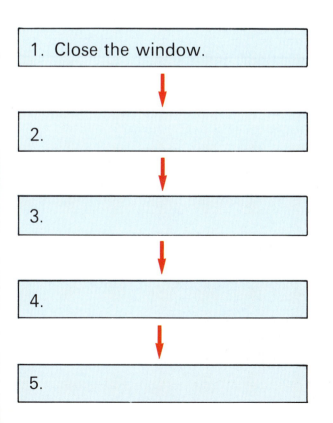

53

DIRECTIONS

Finding the way

Here is a map of City Athletic Stadium. It has four gates.
Gate 1 is in Regent Street, Gates 2 and 3 in Constitution Street and Gate 4 in Park Avenue.

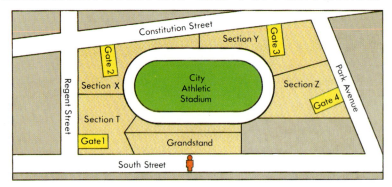

Mr Smith is standing in South Street and he is facing the stadium. What instructions would you give him if he asked you questions 1, 2, 3 and 4?

(Number 1 is done for you, but check to see if it is correct.)

1. Mr Smith: Where is Section Z?
   Your instructions: Turn right, walk to the first corner, turn left down – and enter by Gate –.
   Answer: Turn right, walk to the first corner, turn left down Park Avenue and enter by Gate 4.

2. Mr Smith: Where is Section Y?
   Your instructions: Turn –, walk –, turn – down –, turn – into – and enter by Gate –.

3. Mr Smith: Where is Section T?
   Your instructions: Turn –, walk – – –.

4. Make up instructions for Mr Smith to get to the grandstand.

9. What's missing?
Context Clues including Cloze Procedure

Often we get the message without looking for every detail.

PICTURES

What is missing?

Tom flies his kite
(In this picture the string is missing.)

Tom flies his kite
(In this picture we see the string.)

Copy down the following five pictures and then draw in what is missing.

1. Tom's bicycle   2. Tom's clock   3. Tom's swing   4. Tom's house

5. Tom's street

55

SENTENCES

Missing Words

It is useful to be able to guess correctly what is coming when we are reading.
This will help us to understand what the writer is saying, without having to think about every word he writes. We can play this game first with single sentences.

In each sentence one word is missing, and two suggestions are given in brackets after it. Read the sentence carefully. Look for clues and then try to guess which word has been left out.

Example: Mary and Anne came out – play. (to, and)
   The missing word is *to.*
   The sentence should read: *Mary and Anne came out to play.*

Write down the word which has been missed out in each of the following sentences.

1. The tree ____ very tall.   (fell, grew)
2. The car raced ____ the track.   (round, above)
3. The waiter carried the plates on a ____.   (tray, table)
4. She used soap powder and water to ____ the clothes.   (wash, iron)
5. He could not find his way because it was ____.   (daylight, dark)

PARAGRAPHS

Brave Queen Margaret

Here is a puzzle. You may need to use clues near the beginning or end to find some of the words in the middle. Every tenth word has been missed out, except in the first paragraph where they have been underlined.

Write down a suitable word for each blank in the other paragraphs. (But first of all read the title and the whole story.)

Once, long ago, England had two kings at the same time. It happened in 1461 and the two kings were Henry VI and Edward IV. Naturally each man thought the other <u>man</u> had no right to be king. We call the <u>quarrel</u> between these two kings and their followers the Wars <u>of</u> the Roses. This was because Henry's soldiers were supposed <u>to</u> have worn a red rose as their badge and <u>Edward's</u> soldiers quite often wore a white rose as their <u>badge</u>.

Henry, was a kind man but he was weak-willed. **1** wanted only peace and quiet and when his army **2** beaten by Edward's army he gave up. But Henry's **3** queen, Margaret, went on fighting. When her army was **4** , too, she fled into a forest with her eleven-year-old **5**.

It was getting dark and they soon lost their **6**. Grassy paths wound in and out of the tall **7**. They went this way and that and Margaret did **8** know which path to choose. The dark shadows of **9** trees frightened Margaret's little son and he began to **10**.

"Hush! Hush!" whispered the queen. There were often robbers **11** in the forests of those days and Margaret was **12** a band of outlaws would hear the cries of **13** boy.

They had not gone much farther when they **14** a light ahead. Two men were sitting at a **15**. Margaret could see their shadows and hear the murmur **16** their voices.

(From *Wide Range History*, Book 2, by L. E. Snellgrove)

CLUES TO MEANING
Three men

Do you know the meaning of *gigantic, obese* and *diminutive*?
Perhaps you do not.

Below are pictures of three men and a word to describe each one. Look for clues to the meaning of each word and then do the exercise.

gigantic

obese

diminutive

Write down the underlined words in 1–3 below, like this: 1. gigantic.

Now put beside each the best meaning from the suggestions given.

1. Does <u>gigantic</u> mean: very big, *or* very lazy?

2. Does <u>obese</u> mean: fat, *or* old?

3. Does <u>diminutive</u> mean: very small, *or* very stupid?

Use your dictionary to check whether you have worked out the correct meanings from the picture clues.

Match them up

Look at the following five words:

buccaneer   kayak   sabre   tandem   tepee

Do you know what each one means?

Look at the pictures for clues to the meanings of the words and then do the exercise.

1. tandem

2. sabre

3. buccaneer

4. kayak

5. tepee

Beside each word write down the meaning which matches it.

Words	Meanings
1. tandem	a sword for cutting and thrusting
2. sabre	a pirate
3. buccaneer	Eskimo sealskin canoe
4. kayak	American-Indian tent
5. tepee	a bicycle for two people

(Check up in your dictionary to see if you are correct.)

The Racoon

Look for clues when you read.
Suppose you read: *North America is the home of the racoon.*
Do you know what a racoon is? Is it a fish or a four-legged animal?
Read on: *The racoon is found near rivers and lakes.*
Which clue suggests it is an animal which lives on dry land and not a fish?

Now look at the picture of a racoon at the end of the book (page 64) and answer the question there.

Word Clues

When we have no picture we often find clues in what we read.

This is your Captain speaking

Do you know the meaning of: altitude, destination, renowned?

Read what Captain Muir said to the passengers in his aircraft. Some of the things he said give you clues to the meanings.

1. *Does altitude mean* (a) speed *or* (b) height?
2. *Does destination mean*
   (a) lunch *or* (b) the place to which you are going?
3. *Does renowned mean* (a) forgotten *or* (b) well-known?

Good afternoon. This is the Captain speaking.
We are now flying at an *altitude* of 3 000 metres.
On this short journey we shall not be climbing any higher.
You will arrive at your *destination* in 20 minutes from now.
I am sure you will have a pleasant holiday in the lake-side town. It has always been *renowned* for its excitement and beauty . . . .

10. Take a hint
Inference and Prediction

It helps us to read better if we can use clues to work out what is happening, what is meant, or what is coming next.

Look at the picture.

1. Do you think Mark
   (a) was going for a swim,
   (b) was practising diving, or
   (c) was pushed in?

Which clues made you choose your answer?

INFERENCE

Esther's return

Read the sentence. Answer the question underneath.

Esther arrived back from holiday smiling and sun-tanned, wearing a light cotton dress.

Do you think Esther had been having
(a) dull and rainy weather, *or*
(b) hot and sunny weather?

🧩 Work it out

1. Mr Thomson came up the garden path carrying a hoe and a rake.
   Do you think Mr Thomson was going to
   (a) repair the roof, *or* (b) work in the garden?
   What are the clues?

2. Early in the morning George opened his front door and found a paper bag lying on the path with only one roll left. Three crows were sitting on the lawn and they did not seem able to move.

    George looked along the street. The only person to be seen was the postman delivering letters, but he still had some way to go before he reached George's house.

   Do you think the rolls had been eaten by
   (a) the postman, *or* (b) the crows?
   What are the clues?

3. Mrs Stephen's handbag had disappeared from the dining room table. Apart from herself, there was only old Aunt Agatha in the house and she was asleep in her room.

    The dining room window could only open 15 centimetres. It was impossible for a thief to have come in through that space.

    Mrs Stephen went outside. There she found an old brass curtain rail bent in the shape of a hook, lying outside the dining room window.

   Do you think the handbag was stolen by
   (a) Aunt Agatha, *or* (b) a thief from outside?
   What are the clues?

PREDICTION

Sometimes you can find clues to suggest what is happening, and also to suggest what is going to happen.

The Flood

Look at the pictures and then answer the questions below.

1. Did the rain and floods start during the daytime or during the night? Why do you think so?
2. Do the family sleep downstairs or upstairs? Why do you think so?
3. Write a few sentences to say what you think happened next.

Ann wonders

Ann was walking along Fort Avenue. The street was quiet as it was still very early.

As she passed Mr Hendry's shop, she noticed the door partly open and she glanced in through the window.

"Strange," she thought to herself, "I did not think he opened his shop as early as this. And no sign of him or Mrs Hendry at the counter."

She was even more surprised to see a red car parked across the street. The engine was running and the driver, wearing a hat and dark glasses, looked at her and then gazed towards Mr Hendry's shop.

1. Do you think Mr Hendry did open his shop early that morning?
2. What kind of a person do you think the driver might be?
3. Why do you think he was watching the shop door?
4. Write a few sentences to say what may have happened next.

The Racoon
(continued from page 60)
Write down all the things you now know about a racoon.